D1401314

SLAM DUNK

Basketball Poems Compiled by
Lillian Morrison

Illustrated by Bill James

HYPERION BOOKS FOR CHILDREN   NEW YORK

AS

FIRST EDITION
1   3   5   7   9   10   8   6   4   2

Library of Congress Cataloging-in-Publication Data

Slam dunk: poems about basketball/compiled by Lillian Morrison; illustrated by Bill James–1st ed. p.   cm. Includes index. ISBN 0-7868-0054-2 (trade)–ISBN 0-7868-2042-X (lib. bdg.)–ISBN 0-7868-1060-2 (pbk.) 1. Basketball–Juvenile poetry. 2. Children's poetry, American   I. Morrison, Lillian.   II. James, Bill. PS595.B334S58   1995   811'.54080355–dc20   94-14620 CIP AC

Acknowledgments

Grateful acknowledgment is made to the following people for allowing us to illustrate their likenesses in this book: Patrick Ewing, Jerry West, Shaquille O'Neal, Elgin Baylor, Julius Erving, and Wilt Chamberlain.
For permission to reprint the poems listed below, grateful acknowledgment is made to the following: Diane Ackerman. "Patrick Ewing Takes a Foul Shot" from *Lady Faustus* (William Morrow and Company). Copyright © 1983 by Diane Ackerman. **Richard Armour.** "Offensive Defensive" from *All in Sport*. Copyright © 1972 by Richard Armour. Reprinted by permission of McGraw-Hill, Inc. **Robert P. Tristram Coffin.** Twelve lines from "Hoosier Hoop–La." Reprinted with permission of Macmillan Publishing Company from *Primer for America* by Robert P. Tristram Coffin. Copyright © 1943 by Macmillan Publishing Company, renewed 1971 by Margaret Coffin Halvosa, Mary Alice Westcott, Robert P. Tristram Coffin, Jr., and Richard N. Coffin. **Stephen Dunn.** "Basketball: A Retrospective." By permission of the author. **B. H. Fairchild.** "Shooting." First published in *Quarterly West*. Reprinted by permission of the author. **Mel Glenn.** "Hayes Iverson" from *Class Dismissed II* by Mel Glenn. Text copyright © 1986 by Mel Glenn. Reprinted by permission of Clarion Books/Houghton Mifflin Co. All rights reserved. **Eloise Greenfield.** "Reggie" from *Honey, I Love* by Eloise Greenfield. Text copyright © 1978 by Eloise Greenfield. Reprinted by permission of HarperCollins Publishers. **Edwin A. Hoey.** "Foul Shot." Special permission granted by *Read*® magazine, published by Weekly Reader Corporation. Copyright © renewed 1990, 1962 by Weekly Reader Corporation. **Norbert Krapf.** "Basketball Season Begins" from *Somewhere in Southern Indiana: Poems of Midwestern Origins*. Reprinted by permission of Time Being Books. Copyright © 1993 by Time Being Press, Inc. All rights reserved. **Carl Lindner.** "When I Got It Right" from *The Only Game*. Reprinted by permission of Carl Lindner. **Richard J. Margolis.** "A Trash Can's All Right for Basketball." Eight lines from *Looking for a Place*. Copyright © 1969 by Richard J. Margolis. Reprinted by permission of HarperCollins Publishers, Inc. **William Matthews.** "Oscar Robertson: Peripheral Vision" from *Poetry: Points of Departure*. Reprinted by permission of the author. **Tom Meschery.** "Basketball: A Love Song Because It Is" from *Over the Rim*. Copyright © 1968 by Popular Library. Reprinted by permission of the author. **Bill Pearlman.** "West Is West." First appeared in *Take It to the Hoop*. Reprinted by permission of the author. **Richard Peck.** "Jump Shot." Copyright © 1971 by Richard Peck. **Jack Prelutsky.** "Stringbean Small" from *The New Kid on the Block*. Copyright © 1984 by Jack Prelutsky. Reprinted by permission of Greenwillow Books, a division of William Morrow and Company, Inc. **Marci Ridlon.** "Fernando." Copyright © 1983 by the author and used with her permission. **Roy Scheele.** "Nothing but Net." First published in *Pointing Out the Sky*, Sandhills Press. Copyright © 1985 by Roy Scheele. Reprinted by permission of Mark Sanders, editor of Sandhills Press. **Timothy Steele.** "Practice." First appeared in *Crosscurrents* and is reprinted by permission of the author. **May Swenson.** "Wilt Chamberlain." Copyright © 1988 by May Swenson. Used with permission of the literary estate of May Swenson. **Quincy Troupe.** "A Poem for 'Magic'" from *Weather Reports: New and Selected Poems*. Harlem River Press, New York, N.Y. Copyright © 1991 by Quincy Troupe. **Peter F. Vecsey.** "The Man They Call Dr. J." Reprinted by permission of the author. **Mark Vinz.** "Spring Thaw." First published in *The Place My Words Are Looking For*, edited by Paul B. Janeczko, Orchard Books, 1990. Copyright © 1989 by Mark Vinz. Reprinted by permission of the author.
For permission to reprint the formerly unpublished poems listed below, grateful acknowledgment is made to the following: Charles Comfort. "Michael Jordan." Copyright © 1994 by Charles Comfort. **Ralph Fletcher.** "When the Celtics Lose." Copyright © 1994 by Ralph Fletcher. **Anne Haeusler.** "The Grandstander." Copyright © 1994 by Anne Haeusler. **Robert L. Harrison.** "Against All Odds" and "Where's the Ball?" Copyright © 1994 by Robert L. Harrison. **Myra Cohn Livingston.** "Rehash." Copyright © 1994 by Myra Cohn Livingston. **Walter Dean Myers.** "Deanie McLeanie." Copyright © 1994 by Walter Dean Myers. **William Revas.** "Orlando's Magic" and "Solitary Practice." Copyright © 1994 by William Revas. **Jerry Spinelli.** "Two!" Copyright © 1994 by Jerry Spinelli. **Lillian Morrison.** "The Women's Team at L. Bamberger & Co." Copyright © 1994 by Lillian Morrison. **Jacqueline Sweeney.** "Last Quarter's Last Resort." Copyright © 1994 by Jacqueline Sweeney. **Anita Wintz.** "Zone Defense." Copyright © 1994 by Anita Wintz.
Extensive research and best efforts have failed to locate the following authors or copyright holders of the poems listed below: Charlotte Cardenas Dwyer. "Point Scored." First published in *Sports Poems*, edited by R. R. Knudson and P. K. Ebert, Dell, 1971. **Mark Shechner.** "Elgin Baylor" from *Take It to the Hoop*, edited by Daniel Rudman. North Atlantic Books. Copyright © 1980 by Daniel Rudman.

To Marian Reiner,
for her assists every step of the way
−L. M.

To JoAnn, my wife and best friend,
for all her continued
encouragement and support
−B. J.

Other Books by Lillian Morrison

Poetry
> *The Ghosts of Jersey City*
> *Miranda's Music* (with Jean Boudin)
> *The Sidewalk Racer*
> *Who Would Marry a Mineral?*
> *Overheard in a Bubble Chamber*
> *The Break Dance Kids*
> *Whistling the Morning In*

Poetry Anthologies
> *Sprints and Distances*
> *Rhythm Road*
> *At the Crack of the Bat*

Folk Rhyme Collections
> *Yours Till Niagara Falls*
> *Black Within and Red Without*
> *A Diller, A Dollar*
> *Remember Me When This You See*
> *Touch Blue*
> *Best Wishes, Amen*

CONTENTS

PREFACE

Unlike baseball and football, whose origins go back centuries, basketball is a modern game. It was invented in 1891 by James Naismith, a physical education teacher at a YMCA school (now known as Springfield College) in Springfield, Massachusetts, and the home of the Basketball Hall of Fame. Naismith wanted an indoor game for the winter, so using a soccer ball and two peach baskets, one at each end of the gymnasium, he made up the basic rules as we know them today. He never dreamed that basketball would become such a popular sport, played in almost every corner of the world (even on Mars, or so Robert L. Harrison tells us in his amusing poem "Where's the Ball?").

Basketball is also an exceedingly fast-moving game, exciting to watch and requiring finesse, sheer athletic ability, and above-average stamina to play well, so it is not surprising that poets have been inspired to write about it. The poets here range from unknown fans to Tom Meschery, former forward for the Seattle Supersonics, to established writers such as May Swenson, Quincy Troupe, and Richard Peck. They write, sometimes with humor, about their love for the game; they write about the great pro players; and they write about the action, the intricate team play, the expert moves, the shots, and the suspense of the free throw.

If you have ever tried to shoot a ball through the hoop in a school gym, playground, backyard, or driveway or if you go to games or watch them on television, you will be familiar with some of the emotions expressed and the actions described in these poems. And you will also, I hope, experience–this time through words and rhythms–the fun and drama of this game; the feel and excitement of the enormously popular sport of basketball.

–Lillian Morrison

THE GAME

Shoot it, pass it,
Dribble down the floor.
We want a basket.
Score! Score! Score!

HAYES IVERSON

(Basketball Star)

The score is tied,
Hands smooth with sweat,
God, let the ball
Fall through the net.
I'm on the line,
Shooting a pair,
First one rolls off,
Black–hole despair.
Ball feels heavy,
Bounce it once more,
Slow breath–let it
Drop for the score.
The ball is up,
Universe waits,
The ball
       d
          r
            o
          p
         s
           _____
            in,
           69–68!

Mel Glenn

10

WHEN I GOT IT RIGHT

the ball would lift
light as a wish,
gliding like a blessing
over the rim, pure,
or kissing off glass
into the skirt of net.
Once it began
I couldn't miss.
Even in the falling dark,
the ball, before it left
my hand, was sure.

Carl Lindner

FOUL SHOT

With two 60's stuck on the scoreboard
And two seconds hanging on the clock,
The solemn boy in the center of eyes,
Squeezed by silence,
Seeks out the line with his feet,
Soothes his hands along his uniform,
Gently drums the ball against the floor,
Then measures the waiting net,
Raises the ball on his right hand,
Balances it with his left,
Calms it with fingertips,
Breathes,
Crouches,
Waits,
And then through a stretching of stillness,
Nudges it upward.
The ball slides up and out.
Lands,
Leans,
Wobbles,
Wavers,
Hesitates,
Exasperates,
Plays it coy
Until every face begs with unsounding
   screams—
And then
   And then,
     And then,
Right before ROAR-UP,
Dives down and through.

Edwin A. Hoey

12

13

TWO!

Lost amid
the bleachers' squall
the whispered word
of net to ball.

Jerry Spinelli

FROM HOOSIER HOOP-LA

Hoosiers make a whole religion
Out of a game bred in the bone,
On every farm that bears a boy
There is a strange high altar–stone.

A board set with an iron ring,
And on that ring a bottomless net,
And farm boys toss a big ball through
When suns rise and when suns set.

         *   *   *

Young men reach up high each day,
They stretch so much, they shoot up tall,
They grow long and beautiful,
Cleaving the net–loops with the ball.

Robert P. Tristram Coffin

NOTHING BUT NET

The jump shot? It's all in the wrist
and follow–through, and the timing
of the jump. Of course it's one thing
to hit one in a game of HORSE,
and something else over a guy
that's guarding you. What I like best
is shooting baskets by myself,
warming up gradually until,
at the very height of my jump,
I can tell that it's going in
as the ball leaves my fingertips,
arcing to intercept the air
at the dead center of the goal–
that one split second of eclipse.

Roy Scheele

BASKETBALL SEASON BEGINS

Except for the throng
buzzing in the gymnasium,
the town might seem deserted.
Tonight no one drives
up or down Main Street.
Soon every factory worker
balanced on the edge
of the bleachers will
know as exactly as his
boss leaning back in his
chair seat how each of these
high school athletes measures
up against the heroic
individuals on that yardstick
championship team. Every gas
station attendant will be able
to decree as authoritatively
as the superintendent of schools
at what point the new coach's
back deserves to be patted
or his throat summarily slit.
On Monday morning, mayor
and minister alike will inform
their followers exactly why
this team will sputter or soar.
Every native wedged into
this sweaty brick building
has wagered his small town
heritage on the outcome
of this season. The town
has lain dormant for many
a month; at the opening tip–
off it roars itself awake.

Norbert Krapf

JUMP SHOT

Lithe, quicker than the ball itself;
Spinning through the blocking forearms,
Hands like stars, spread to suspend
The ball from five, and only five,
Magic fingerprints.

The rebound resounding down the pole
And into asphalt, pounded hard by sneakers
Raggedier than the missing–tooth grimaces.

Grimaces. No smiles here. Concentration.
Movement. The calculation.
The arch–back leap. And off the rim again.
Once in ten the satisfying swoosh.

And no time wasted to enjoy it.
Grasp that globe and keep it dribbling:
Elbows were meant for eyesockets;
Work it up higher than hands,
Higher than the grab of gravity.

Working, each man for himself,
Yet neatly, neatly weaving in the pattern.

Richard Peck

19

HOOPING IT UP

When you're up, you're up,
When you're down, you're down.
When you're up against our team
You're spinning all around.

FERNANDO

Fernando has a basketball.
He tap, tap, taps it down the hall,
then leaps up high and shoots with care.
The fact a basket isn't there,
he totally dismisses.
He says he never misses.
My crazy friend Fernando.

Marci Ridlon

OFFENSIVE DEFENSIVE

Our team, though quite tall,
Simply can't score at all,
An almost impossible task, it.
What makes it so hard
Is their five–foot–five guard
Who sits up on top of the basket.

Richard Armour

STRINGBEAN SMALL

Stringbean Small was tall and trim,
basketball seemed meant for him,
at eight foot four, a coach's dream,
and yet he failed to make the team.

It seems at practice, Stringbean Small
began to chew the basketball,
the coach screamed, "Stop! Don't nibble it!
I wanted you to *dribble* it!"

Jack Prelutsky

WHERE'S THE BALL?

They found the hoops
under the sands of Mars
near a pile
of basketball cards.

The court stretched
for at least a mile.
When the Lakers heard
they clapped and smiled.

The scorebook said
there was a foul.
Two Redmen had left
by the nearest canal.

By the placing
of the whitened bones,
it seemed the ref
had died alone.

No one knows
which side won.
Maybe those Martians
were just having fun?

Robert L. Harrison

SOLITARY PRACTICE

Dribble, dribble and shoot.
I just dunked a beaut.
Fast break down the floor,
Fake a pass, shoot once more.
In again. Perfect aim.
Why can't I do this in a game?

William Revas

A TRASH CAN'S ALL RIGHT FOR BASKETBALL

A trash can's all right for basketball
but not if it's empty.
Every time you sink one
you have to lean way over
to get the ball.
It's hard on the ribs.
If you don't want to lean,
keep your city clean.

Richard J. Margolis

THE GRANDSTANDER

The score was tied
with a minute to go.
Ball caught at midcourt–
she poised for the throw,
a two–handed shot,
a perfect long loop.
Unbelievable!
Right into the hoop.
She should have passed
but all the same
her team forgave her
for winning the game.

Anne Haeusler

REGGIE

It's summertime
And Reggie doesn't live here anymore
He lives across the street
Spends his time with the round ball
Jump, turn, shoot
Through the hoop
Spends his time with arguments
    and sweaty friends
And not with us
He's moved away
Comes here just to eat and sleep
    and sometimes pat my head
Then goes back home
To run and dribble and jump and stretch
And stretch
And shoot
Thinks he's Kareem
And not my brother

Eloise Greenfield

POINT SCORED

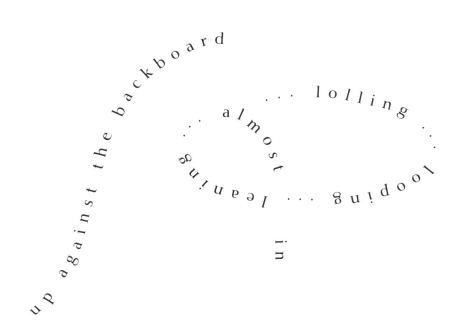

Charlotte Cardenas Dwyer

ZONE DEFENSE

"Hey, stay outta my space
 I'll give you a hand in the face."
   Zig–Zag, ZAP!

"Hey, I'm here to defend.
 Your motion, I'm gonna suspend."
   Zig–Zag, ZAP!

Anita Wintz

THE PROS

We're on the gym floor.
The gym floor's hot.
You can't beat us
With the team we've got.

PATRICK EWING TAKES A FOUL SHOT

Ewing sweating,
molding the ball
with spidery hands,
packing it, packing it,
into a snowball's
chance of a goal,
rolling his shoulders
through a silent earthquake,
rocking from one foot
to the other, sweating,
bouncing it, oh, sweet
honey, molding it,
packing it tight,
he fires:

floats it up on one palm
as if surfacing
from the clear green Caribbean
with a shell
whose roar wraps around him,
whose surf breaks
deep into his arena
where light and time
and pupils jump
because he jumps

Diane Ackerman

AGAINST ALL ODDS

The age of "Magic"
is yielding,
slowly off court,
into the shadows
like fingertips
grabbing at
loose laces.

But "Magic"
will forever smile,
and play against
the sirens' song,
and will not
foul out until
the final point
is made.

Robert L. Harrison

A POEM FOR "MAGIC"

For Earvin "Magic" Johnson, Donnell Reid & Richard Franklin

take it to the hoop, "magic" johnson
take the ball dazzling down the open lane
herk & jerk & raise your six feet nine inch
frame into air sweating screams of your neon name
"magic" johnson, nicknamed "windex" way back
    in high school
cause you wiped glass backboards so clean
where you first juked & shook
wiled your way to glory
a new style fusion of shake & bake energy
using everything possible, you created your own space
to fly through–any moment now, we expect your wings
to spread feathers for that spooky take off of yours–
then shake & glide, till you hammer home
a clotheslining deuce off glass
now, come back down with a reverse hoodoo gem
off the spin, & stick it in sweet, popping nets, clean
from twenty feet, right–side

put the ball on the floor, "magic"
slide the dribble behind your back, ease it deftly
between your bony, stork legs, head bobbing everwhichaway
up & down, you see everything on the court
off the high, yoyo patter, stop & go dribble, you shoot
a threading needle rope pass, sweet home to kareem
cutting through the lane, his skyhook pops cords
now lead the fastbreak, hit worthy on the fly
now, blindside a behind the back pinpointpass for two more
off the fake, looking the other way
you raise off balance into space
sweating chants of your name, turn, 180 degrees
off the move, your legs scissoring space, like a swimmer's
yoyoing motion, in deep water, stretching out now toward free

flight, you double–pump through human trees, hang in place
slip the ball into your left hand
then deal it like a las vegas card dealer
off squared glass, into nets, living up to your singular nickname
so "bad", you cartwheel the crowd towards frenzy
wearing now your electric smile, neon as your name

in victory, we suddenly sense your glorious uplift
your urgent need to be champion
& so we cheer, rejoicing with you, for this quicksilver, quicksilver
    quicksilver
moment of fame, so put the ball on the floor again, "magic"
juke & dazzle, shake & bake down the lane
take the sucker to the hoop, "magic" johnson,
re–create reverse hoodoo gems off the spin,
deal alley–oop–dunk–a–thon–magician passes
now, double–pump, scissor, vamp through space
hang in place & put it all up in the sucker's face, "magic"
johnson, & deal the roundball, like the juju man that you am
like the sho–nuff shaman man that you am
"magic", like the sho–nuff spaceman, you am

      Quincy Troupe

WEST IS WEST

Whenever stardom in light
I craved the sharing of
comes to mind there is
the image of Jerry West
Hitting a 20 foot jumper
with an ingenious precision
made one think
he was always right there:
scoring at the edge of the key

Bill Pearlman

OSCAR ROBERTSON: PERIPHERAL VISION

They clear the left side for him.
An eye–fake, dip and ripple
of a shoulder, he runs his man
into a pick. He's done this so many times
it hurts him the right way.
The ball blooms away from his wrist.
The body is most vulnerable
when it claims space,
shadows in the moist
and painfully kept open
corners of his eyes.

William Matthews

MICHAEL JORDAN

Performs his acrobatics
in the air, and scores.
He likes to dump 'em in.

Driving to the hoop,
he soars, and hovers there
up above the rim.

His hang time, slams and dunks
make history. That's why
they name those sneakers after him.

Charles Comfort

ELGIN BAYLOR

                you had to see it
the leap
        sudden
        selfgenerated
                    the moment
bursting
        into golden petals
        arch
        of the neck

ex–
tension of the arm

you just had
to see
        the feint
                    leading
        to a takeoff
        arms
        lifting
                    the whole flower
glorious
and the great re–
                    lease
                    of energy

you had
        to see
Baylor
        before his knees went

        how
        he could
        dance

                    Mark Shechner

41

THE MAN THEY CALL DR. J.

doesn't just shoot
the normal jump shot
but catapults himself
from the floor and lofts
his shots from somewhere
in the rafters, doesn't
just reject his opponent's
shot, he skyjacks it,
doesn't merely dunk the ball,
he suffocates the rim with
an explosive, forced-entry
slam-jam! The man soars,
hand outstretched like
a giant derrick, vacuums
the ball to his fingertips
drawing it safely to his
chest in midair. Then in a
bewildering flash, he's
charging downcourt, shifting
gears, changing directions,
hustling past opponents,
driving toward the basket.
Suddenly he's airborne again,
huge right hand cupping
the ball as one would cup a
grapefruit. Surrounded by
leaping bodies, he goes higher
and higher, until–WHOOSH!–
another impossible two-pointer.

Pete Vecsey

43

WILT CHAMBERLAIN

Wilt was so built
he could give it a tilt
over the rim
hardly higher than him.

Does Wilty feel guilty
he's not that trim
in girth and limb
as when he was slim?

Old age is grim.

Now, much like Joe
DiMaggio
Wilty is seen
on the TV screen
with an easy laugh
folding in half.

He's doing a plug
for the Volkswagen Bug
to prove it's wide
enough, tall, and more so,
for Wilt's famous torso
to fit inside.

May Swenson

ORLANDO'S MAGIC

I know a rookie
beyond compare.
He's got the height,
he's got the flair,
the power, the moves.
Opponents, beware!
Shaquille O'Neal.
That's a poem right there.

William Revas

WHEN THE CELTICS LOSE

My face has crusted,
bone dust in my throat
from grinding these teeth;

I could calmly hammer
an iron stake
into the heart of this tv.

Mom says that games teach us
to lose with dignity and grace,
to grow wiser in the process.

I have heard all that
and still all this bone dust
clogging my constricted throat.

The day is empty as an insect husk.
I race through a cold forest,
eat wind until my lungs are torn.

Wish I could sleep out all night,
just me, the tall quiet trees,
the sound of one Bird's sad song.

Ralph Fletcher

BASKETBALL: A LOVE SONG BECAUSE IT IS

I will always remember:
the din of Madison Square Garden
filled with Saturday night people,
the sadness of a loss
or the gaiety of victory
that tomorrow could change,
traveling the early hour jets
cards shuffling
endless insomnia,
tired muscles,
bawdy conversation,
pointless anxiety
over yesterday's statistics,
the tunneled echoes
of airports at four A.M.
and the moment when
with absolute certainty
the ball slipped soundlessly from my fingers
backspinning beauty through the net.

Tom Meschery

PLAYERS ALL

To the right, center, forward, guard,
Get that ball, it's not hard.
Shoot it high, pass it low,
Come on, guys, LET'S GO!

DEANIE McLEANIE

Deanie McLeanie is a basketball genie
Six foot seven from his sneakers to his beanie

He wears a fourteen jersey and a fifteen shoe
And there's nothing on the court that the kid can't do

He can scoop, he can loop
He can put it through the hoop

He can ram, he can slam
He can do the flying jam

He can tap, he can rap
He can snatch it with a slap

He can dunk, he can plunk
He can stop and make the junk

He can shake, he can bake
He can lose you with a fake

He can pin, he can win
He can do the copter spin

Cause Deanie McLeanie's a basketball genie
Six foot seven from his sneakers to his beanie

He wears a fourteen jersey and a fifteen shoe
And there's nothing on the court that the kid can't do.

Walter Dean Myers

PRACTICE

The basketball you walk around the court
Produces a hard, stinging, clean report.
You pause and crouch, and, after feinting, swoop
Around a ghost defender to the hoop
And rise and lay the ball in off the board.
Solitude, plainly, is its own reward.

The game that you've conceived engrosses you.
The ball rolls off, you chase it down, renew
The dribble to the level of your waist.
Insuring that a sneaker's tightly laced,
You kneel–then, up again, wave easily
Through obstacles that you alone can see.

And so I drop the hands I'd just now cupped
To call you home. Why should I interrupt?
Can I be sure that dinner's ready yet?
A jumpshot settles, snapping through the net;
The backboard's stanchion keeps the ball in play,
Returning it to you on the ricochet.

Timothy Steele

THE WOMEN'S TEAM AT L. BAMBERGER & CO.

Our best forward
wasn't very tall
but made up for it
in speed, spunk and
spring in the knees.
She could almost slam–dunk.
Proud, in our snazzy
silver shorts, maroon tops,
we ran and sweated
in those drafty gyms
(seats mostly empty)
somehow always playing
against bigger, rougher teams,
tough girls who shoved
and elbowed, but Maggie's
fakes and pivots, charges
down the floor, layups,
jumpers, onehanders
would fire us up, and the
few times we did win,
the bare locker rooms,
as we showered and dressed,
rang with our rejoicing
and when we emerged, heading
for the bus, each of us
at least two inches taller,
the frosty air outside
seemed to greet us with kisses.

Lillian Morrison

53

SPRING THAW

Up and down March streets
small boys with basketballs
beneath torn nets or none at all
and Mother calling supper

just beyond the porch door's slap
the thudding ball is mud–caked
soaked from puddles, fingers numb
with only time for one last jump

shot, snowflakes fluttering
between the streetlights blinking
time for one more shot one
last time Mother calling more!

Mark Vinz

BASKETBALL: A RETROSPECTIVE

My ethics were
    a good pair of hands,
      a good move
when things were difficult.

An exceptional man
    could change direction
      in the air,
could thread a needle.

Stephen Dunn

LAST QUARTER'S LAST RESORT

That guard is like
a Bull in sneakers
snorting fast
down center court.

The other guard's
a huffing Rhino
puffing past
in bulging shorts.

The forwards are
Giraffes in jerseys
Center is
an owl–eyed Stork.

And I am just
a bug–eyed Freshman;
can't outzone
or full court press them.
can't outpivot,
pass, cavort

can't outdribble
or outshoot them,
can't outhuff,
outpuff or snort.

But I outsweat,
outshake, outwhine them.
I do all but
wine and dine them!

I'm last quarter's
last resort.
And if this weren't enough . . .

I'm short.

Jacqueline Sweeney

56

REHASH

Like it
was a greased pig,
back and forth, back and forth,
we handled it, Ford working
down the

left side
sneaking behind
Kirk, and then, whambo,
wouldn't you know the ball squirted
out of

my hands,
Ames fouled, Hobbs was
benched, and even though they
pounded us, we played good enough
to win.

Myra Cohn Livingston

SHOOTING

Dusk was best. Searching
for the perfect shot,
I'd dribble, pivot, jump,
let go, and watch the ball
float full–moon across
a darkening sky, then sink
into the strings that hugged,
then dropped it to the ground.
Far into the night
I stayed, moving through
the backyard gloom, a ghost
even to myself, shooting
where I couldn't see.
The sounds of bounce and jump
echoed from the house,
followed by the silence
of the ball's long flight.
Going up, each time
my body felt itself
curve evenly from toe
to shoulder, through arms
and fingertips that sensed
the arc the ball would take
before the quick whisper
somewhere in the dark.

B. H. Fairchild

59

NOTES ON THE PLAYERS

Preface–Tom Meschery, the popular forward for the Seattle Supersonics from 1967 to 1971, was born in China, the son of Russian émigrés. The family settled in this country when he was a boy. He has played basketball since he was 12 and was a high school, college, and AAU all–American. He is the only pro basketball player who can boast a published book of his own poetry, and he now teaches high school English in California.

"Reggie"–Kareem Abdul–Jabbar was born Lew Alcindor, Jr., but changed his name in 1970, having converted to Islam. He starred at Power Memorial High School in New York City and later at UCLA. Eventually, as the seven–foot–two center for the Milwaukee Bucks and the Los Angeles Lakers, he became the all–time NBA leader in scoring (38,387 career points scored) with the help of his unblockable skyhook. Among his other NBA records are most seasons played (20), most career games (1,560), and most career field goals (15,837). He was named the NBA's MVP six times, another record.

"Patrick Ewing Takes a Foul Shot"–Patrick Ewing, the seven–foot center for the New York Knicks, was born in Jamaica and came to the United States at age nine. He starred at Georgetown University, where he was known as the Hoya Destroya, helping his team to the NCAA championship game three times in four years. The Knicks' first pick (and first overall) in the 1985 college draft, he was named Rookie of the Year in 1986 despite injuries and eventually turned this last–place team around in his fourth season. He continues to be a high–scoring mainstay of the team.

"A Poem for 'Magic' " and "Against All Odds"–Earvin "Magic" Johnson, Jr., is considered by some to be the greatest all–around player ever. As their six–foot–nine point guard, he helped the Los Angeles Lakers win five NBA championships in the 1980s. With his no–look pass and wonderful moves, he held the NBA record for assists. In November 1991, Johnson disclosed that he was HIV–positive. In spite of this, he played on the 1992 U.S. Olympic team and made one NBA appearance at the All–Star Game in Orlando, where he was named the game's MVP. Now retired, he has also been honored for his many contributions to charitable causes.

"West Is West"–Jerry West is a Hall of Fame guard who played for the Los Angeles Lakers in the 1960s and the early 1970s. At six foot two and a half, considered short for a basketball player, he was a great playmaker and was known as Mr. Clutch. He ranks among the all-time leaders with 25,192 points scored during his 14-year career, a scoring average of 27 points per game (fourth best), and also ranks among the best in free throws, field goals, and assists. He was an all-NBA first teamer 10 times and played in a total of 12 All-Star Games.

"Orlando's Magic"–Shaquille "Shaq" O'Neal, seven foot one and 294 pounds, is the sensational young center for the Orlando Magic. He first showed his remarkable talents at Louisiana State University, where he simultaneously led the Southeastern Conference in scoring (27.6 points per game), rebounding (14.7), field-goal percentage (62.8%), and blocked shots (140)– the only college player ever to do so. He was named Rookie of the Year in 1993 and promises to be one of the outstanding centers in basketball history.

"Michael Jordan"–Michael Jordan, the six-foot-six Chicago Bulls superstar, with his soaring leaps and tremendous scoring ability, is considered by many the most exciting player ever to play. Stardom began at the University of North Carolina, and after the 1984–85 season, his first in the pros, he was named Rookie of the Year. He was an NBA MVP three times and won Olympic gold medals in 1984 and 1992. He holds the record for career scoring average with more than 32.2 points per game. He retired from basketball suddenly in October 1993.

"Elgin Baylor"–Elgin Baylor, the six-foot-five Laker, was one of the great for-wards of all time. He was named Rookie of the Year in 1959 and from then on was an All-Star, for 10 years in a row. Noted for his ability to soar, (he seemed to float in midair), he racked up 23,149 points and had a scoring average of 27.4 points per game in his 14-year career. He is in the Hall of Fame.

"The Man They Call Dr. J."–Julius "Dr. J" Erving, six foot six and a half, is a basketball legend because of his spectacular play–his "tomahawk dunk," his spins, whirls, and leaps. He starred in the playgrounds of Roosevelt, New

York, as well as in high school, in college, and for five years in the ABA. But it was as a forward for the Philadelphia 76ers that he dazzled fans for 11 seasons, during which he played in every All-Star Game. He was MVP for the ABA from 1974 to 1976 and for the NBA in 1981, and he was recently named to the Hall of Fame.

"Wilt Chamberlain"–Wilt Chamberlain, the seven-foot-one center and Hall of Famer known as the Big Dipper, was a tremendously talented offensive player and holds more NBA records than any other player. He played for the Philadelphia Warriors, the 76ers, and the Los Angeles Lakers and was named NBA MVP four times. He also led the league in scoring seven straight years. Among his records are most points scored in a season (4,029); most field goals in a season (1,597) and in a game (36); and most rebounds in a season (2,149), in a game (55), and in a career (23,924). In 1961–62 he averaged 50.4 points per game. Probably his most truly unsurpassable record is his 100 points scored in one game.

"Oscar Robertson: Peripheral Vision"–Oscar "the Big O" Robertson, a six-foot-five guard, was an all-American at the University of Cincinnati, then played with the Cincinnati Royals for much of his pro career, racking up a 30.5 points-per-game scoring average with them. His career average is 25.7 points per game. Before the 1970–71 season he was traded to the Milwaukee Bucks, who that year won the league championship in only their third season. Kareem was known as Mr. Inside on this team, Oscar as Mr. Outside. He is in second place all time with 7,694 free throws and in third with 9,887 assists. He is in the Hall of Fame.

"When the Celtics Lose"–Larry Bird, the six-foot-nine forward for the Boston Celtics and a great all-around player throughout the 1980s, was an exceptional shooter, passer, and rebounder. He was the NBA's Rookie of the Year for 1979–80, leading his team in scoring, rebounding, and minutes played. He also led the Celtics to many championship titles and was the league's MVP three times in a row. He was noted for his one-hand push shot and long-range jump shot, and in 1989–90, he led the league with his .930 free-throw percentage. He retired in August 1992.